UGLY MUGS

PETA BRADY

CURRENCY PRESS
SYDNEY

GRIFFIN
THEATRE
COMPANY

CURRENCY PLAYS

First published in 2014
by Currency Press Pty Ltd,
PO Box 2287, Strawberry Hills, NSW, 2012, Australia
enquiries@currency.com.au
www.currency.com.au

in association with Griffin Theatre Company

Copyright: © Peta Brady, 2014.

COPYING FOR EDUCATIONAL PURPOSES

The Australian *Copyright Act 1968* (Act) allows a maximum of one chapter or 10% of this book, whichever is the greater, to be copied by any educational institution for its educational purposes provided that that educational institution (or the body that administers it) has given a remuneration notice to Copyright Agency Limited (CAL) under the Act.
For details of the CAL licence for educational institutions contact CAL, Level 15, 233 Castlereagh Street, Sydney, NSW, 2000; tel: within Australia 1800 066 844 toll free; outside Australia 61 2 9394 7600; fax: 61 2 9394 7601; email: info@copyright.com.au

COPYING FOR OTHER PURPOSES

Except as permitted under the Act, for example a fair dealing for the purposes of study, research, criticism or review, no part of this book may be reproduced, stored in a retrieval system, or transmitted in any form or by any means without prior written permission. All enquiries should be made to the publisher at the address above.

Any performance or public reading of *Ugly Mugs* is forbidden unless a licence has been received from the author or the author's agent. The purchase of this book in no way gives the purchaser the right to perform the play in public, whether by means of a staged production or a reading. All applications for public performance should be addressed to the author c/- Currency Press.

Cataloguing-in-publication data for this title is available from the National Library of Australia website: www.nla.gov.au

Typeset by Dean Nottle for Currency Press.
Cover photograph by Brett Boardman. Cover design by RE:.
Front cover shows Peta Brady.

Currency Press acknowledges the Traditional Owners of the Country on which we live and work. We pay our respects to all Aboriginal and Torres Strait Islander Elders, past and present.

Contents

Ugly Mugs 1

Theatre Program at the end of the playtext

AUTHOR'S NOTES

Ugly Mugs is a grassroots program. An initiative of the prostitute collective of Victoria, started in 1986.

It is a tool used by sex workers to report aggresive clients. It is a crime prevention strategy. A way of keeping each other safe.

Thank you to those who have contributed to this piece along the way. I have badgered many a friend, colleague, client, cast member and stranger. You have provided me with content and dramaturgy for which I am forever grateful.

Special thanks to Marion Potts for taking a chance on this one: for commissioning the work and her ongoing support throughout the entire process. I'm feelin' the privilege. And to Lee Lewis at Griffin Theatre Company for also taking a risk on this new work: programming it and being so encouraging.

This story is inspired by those who endure violence on the street and, at worst, those who have lost their lives. It is not about any one person. It is unfortunately the story of many.

PB

Ugly Mugs was first produced by Malthouse Theatre and Griffin Theatre Company at the Merlyn Theatre, Melbourne, on 16 May 2014, with the following cast:

SON	Harry Boland
WORKING GIRL / MUM	Peta Brady
DOC / MUG	Steve Le Marquand
FOOTY GIRL	Sara West

Director, Marion Potts
Set & Costume Design, Michael Hankin
Lighting Design, Lucy Birkinshaw
Composer & Sound Design, Darrin Verhagen

CHARACTERS

WORKING GIRL, street sex worker, bubbly, full of life
MUM, dry, working-class battler
SON, wayward teenager
FOOTY GIRL, tough teenage girl, a natural with the football
DOC, kind, clinical, in his own head
MUG, a man, ordinary

SETTING

This story takes place all one day / night.

Scenes take place in a morgue and a juvenile prison cell. Memory takes us to a car, carpark, suburban park.

This play went to press before the end of rehearsals and may differ from the play as performed.

MORGUE

WORKING GIRL *is on a slab.*

WORKING GIRL: Really nice white teeth. Black Mercedes. I'd been daydreamin' 'bout a car with a heater and up rocks this five-seater four-wheel drive with electronically heated leather seats. Seats that made me feel dirty even though I wasn't. But ya could never be clean as them. Never have that brand-new smell. Some kinda cologne. Can't think but it stink. Baby seat in the back. Pink blanket on the floor. Couldn't see his eyes cos of his shades. Silver diamond earring. In his left ear. Hat. Not a beanie, a cap. Letters on the front. C somethin'. Cycles. Circles. Circus. Citipower. I donno, it started with C. Remember cos it was a capital. Big. He wasn't… tall. But not short. Medium. No tatts I saw. Didn't get the rego. Not a mo, but stubble, like tryin' to grow. Like a five o'clock shadow. But I know it was later. He wore jeans. T-shirt but with a collar. Red. Stripes. Sneakers. White. Nike. Remember clockin' the tick thinkin' it was a sign. Mark of approval. Things were gonna go well. He smoked menthol. Cos I scabbed one. Taste like shit. Car smelt like Glen 20 and the doors locked electronically from his side.

The sound of car doors locking.

DOC: Female.

36.

Caucasian.

Brown wavy past-the-shoulder-length hair.

Blue eyes.

WORKING GIRL: Who would you choose to be if you could be anyone? He ask.

Me was alright. Me. He giggled then went quiet for a while. Put on the radio. Took some back roads. We get there he goes, 'D'ya know where ya are?'

Carpark. His choice. Wasn't my usual routine. But the cops were out and I didn't have time to chat. My frozen face started to thaw soon as I opened the door and my feet were lovin' me for this score. Close to the city cos I saw it out the window as we sped up the ramp and parked lookin' out over everything. Lots of new construction goin' on and a big crane. Says Gro something. All lit up in lights. Con! Yeah. Cos I play with it in me head. Gro Con. Think of big growing cons. Huge grown con men.

DOC: Silver eagle ring left hand. Fourth proximal digit.

Faux fur coat.

Singlet.

Black satin slip.

Black cotton bra.

Short black skirt.

Boy's-style black boxer underpants not her size. Cotton.

One long boot. Left. Black. With heel.

WORKING GIRL: He offers me some whisky from a small bottle he pulled outta the glove box. Wouldn't normally take a drink but he seemed like a nice guy. Warped the lights to grog'on . Sign in the sky. Talkin' at me. The moon's just there. Face all full. Starin' at me. Right out the window. Lookin' straight at me. Glarin', it's starin', shine on me.

Have you ever been this close to it? He ask.

Feel like I can practically reach out and touch it, grab it. Big ball. Jus' throw myself out there and catch it. Do it in me head. Feel it's burning thud on me chest as I fly through the sky an' snatch it. Hear the roar. Screamin' at the dark for more light.

DOC: What happened next?

WORKING GIRL: Sucked his cock.

DOC: Right.

WORKING GIRL: Didn't pick me up for me personality. Just lucked that in.

DOC: Right. Yes.

WORKING GIRL: Nah, never got the vibe he drive me out there cos he wanna swap recipes for banana bread. That's a different guy. I'd never seen this one.

DOC: So. Right. Then you?

WORKING GIRL: Watched a DVD. If he's payin' I'm stayin'. He's next to me. Talkin' at the [*making an electronic sound*] zzzzzztttt built-in TV. Fuck me.

   Watching porn…

Bit fat this slut. He say. But licks his lip anyway.

Big sinkhole between her thighs.

See it?

She's dressed as a nun. The cop with his greased-up baton an' double-barrelled gun. The fireman's hose up her bum. I'd seen this one. In'll come a dude in a priest outfit thinkin' a bible gonna fit.

   She lies back down on the slab. DOC *notices an 'Ugly Mugs' booklet poking out of her boot. He removes it.*

DOC: 'Ugly Mugs'?

   He starts to read the 'Ugly Mugs' report.

CELL

SON: Wish I never saw it.
    Better than me nearly.
    Thought it musta been a fluke. Watched it for a while. The way it sway an' it play the wind. Knew exactly how the ball'd ride it. Sendin' it surfin'. Filled up me eyes with it.
    Bang bang bang it just kept nailin' it. Thwack.
    Must have balls I think and creep in get a closer look.
    Some freak I was expectin'. Maybe three eyes somethin' weird.
    Not normal for a girl, so it can't be one. Not a normal one.
    She has two eyes. Not three. Neither of 'em see me.
    Didn't plan it. Just did it. Smack. Skimmed off the air. Lands fair on her forehead. She falls down. Holding her head.
    Checkin' her hand, to see how much of her head's in it.
    Looks up like none of it. Like it was a leaf, some feather just fall in her hair.
    Can hear the sound my heart pound tryna shut it down so she don't look round.
    Somethin' not right. Not normal.
    Can't take my eyes back. They're stuck on her.
    If I was a butterfly, I'd have people in me stomach.
    She's all alone.
    In some trance.
    I'm keeping quiet as I can.
    Never seen anything like it.
    She walks and disappears into the toilets.
    Wait. She come out, I walk past like I just got there. But my eyes musta still been stuck cos she spots the stare. Glares. Then looks away.
    Like she shy but I don't buy it.
    Not with a kick like that.

You got brothers?
The sound of a ball being booted: Thwack!
Boom on my chest.

FOOTY GIRL: Marked me.

SON: Wrapped me arms around it.

FOOTY GIRL: You got sisters?

SON: Huh?

FOOTY GIRL: Gonna give it back?

SON: What?

FOOTY GIRL: Ball.

SON: Oh, line her up and… I donno.
Didn't really think about it.
Snap. Screw punt.

FOOTY GIRL: Mongrel punt.

SON: Banana.

FOOTY GIRL: Rainmaker.

SON: What?

FOOTY GIRL: High enough to stir the sky but not coverin' much ground. Like your blades weren't workin'. That was more a floater cos you got your shin involved.

FOOTY GIRL kicks sharp and direct. Hits SON's chest hard.

SON: Stab pass. Punches the air out my lungs. I try get me blades goin', kick a beauty, give me time to get me breathe back. Thwack.

SON kicks.

It was a screamer. She marks it one hand facin' the sun. Game on. But she starts walkin' away. As if it's done. She'd won. Starts to run.

Swings round. Lines up, steps in, has a crack.

Thwack. Never seen a torpedo with so much spin. Every little move she made, up to it endin' up on her sneaker at the exact angle. Boom. Thought it was never gonna land. Straight towards the sun. Looked like it was gonna clear it. Go straight over it. A missile. Smash. We freeze. Shards fly everywhere. Walk away. Like we both seen nothin'. Like we both just got there.

FOOTY GIRL: You got my bag?

SON: Didn't you mind it?

FOOTY GIRL: Why would I mind it?

SON: Where'd you leave it?

FOOTY GIRL: Just…

SON: How long ago?
When you see it last?

FOOTY GIRL: I'm thinking.

SON: Not safe.

FOOTY GIRL: What?

SON: To just leave it. Someone must've…

FOOTY GIRL: Taken it? Even though it's not theirs to take.

SON: Shoulda come in closer smothered it.

FOOTY GIRL: What?

SON: The ball. Was a shit kick.

FOOTY GIRL: It was just over there. You know where it is. Can tell.

SON: Don't.

FOOTY GIRL: You're weird.

SON: What do ya mean?

FOOTY GIRL: Weird.

SON: I'm weird? I didn't.

FOOTY GIRL: Was a really good shot.

SON: What was?

FOOTY GIRL: The rock. Right above the temple. 99 outta 100 I give ya.

SON: What for?

FOOTY GIRL: Well, it wasn't a perfect score. Still some work to do on your aim.

SON: You're the one jus' kick the ball through a light.

FOOTY GIRL: Did you hide it?

SON: What?

FOOTY GIRL: My bag. Keep me here longer lookin' for it? Get another shot at me.

SON: Why would I do that?

FOOTY GIRL: Cos you like me or somethin'.

SON: No I don't. I mean no I didn't.

FOOTY GIRL: So you do. But you didn't.

SON: I never.

FOOTY GIRL: Woulda been clever.

SON: You think I done it?

FOOTY GIRL: Hit me? Or taken it?

SON: Both. Either.

FOOTY GIRL: Everybody capable of anything. If they think of it. They can do it.

SON: Never think of doin' that.

FOOTY GIRL: No-one else about to think it.

SON: A bird mighta dropped somethin'. Or a little chunk musta fell off a star or somethin' weird.

FOOTY GIRL: But they not out.

SON: Jus' because ya can't see 'em don't mean they ain't there. A bit of meteor. The sky jus' spat one out. God's dummy hit ya in the head.

FOOTY GIRL: Aimed at me?

SON: Cos there's no-one else we see.

MORGUE

DOC: Mug and worker negotiated service. Mug stated politely that he liked to be dominant. Mug offered worker Mogadon. Worker declined. Mug wanted to pay with jewellery. Worker declined. Mug became verbally and physically aggressive during service and placed worker in headlock. She began choking. She requested he stop. He refuses request.

WORKING GIRL: They not all bad. If they are they end up in there. Fill out the form.

DOC: Where did you get this?

WORKING GIRL: What he do to ya? What he look like? What he say? How you got away? Then /

DOC: Go to police?

WORKING GIRL: No-one gonna run to someone they've been hidin' from all day. They got special laws just for us. We are other. South Africa cops pepper spray ya in the vagina. Saw it on YouTube. Ain't nobody got time for dat! Nah, it's typed up somewhere else. Passed round. So we all don't go with the same psycho. I donno. Nothin' bad never happened to me. Got that copy from Jackie.

DOC: Who?

WORKING GIRL: Told the cops her name was Jackie Russell. Cos she's got one. A Jack Russell. First thing that pop in her head, she said. Was funny as fuck. So it stuck.

DOC: No names.

WORKING GIRL: Her workin' name's Sarah, real name's Kelly. I call her Jackie. She calls me tissue tits. Piss herself when I show her how I make my tits look bigger. She's who I call if I'm ever in trouble. Call each other if need be. She mostly just text me food she eatin'. Breakfast lunch tea. Fuck.

Told me 'bout the dude with the red hatchback. Iced up and aggro on. And the three chicks in a blue commodore one windscreen wiper drivin' round throwin' eggs. Hit one of the trans workers in the shoulder and her friend on the legs. Bruises and cuts. Yellin' out the window, 'ya dirty sluts'.

They visit the boys too. There was only one out. Wouldna been much fun for him.

I read up to the purple ute. Picked up worker alone took her home but his friends followed. Black pulsar. Wheels looked too big for the car. Tinted windows. Held her down. Took it in goes.

Didn't read it all. Got a job.

DOC: Why street?

WORKING GIRL: Why not? Not out to bother no-one. Do an honest day's work. Go home.

DOC: You enjoy it?

WORKING GIRL: Why not?

DOC: Strangers' bodies.

WORKING GIRL: Strange heads more the worry.

DOC *is cutting off her clothes. Pulls out a wad of tissues.*

DOC: Tissues.

WORKING GIRL: Told ya.

DOC *continues to cut through her clothing revealing a large tattoo on her chest.*

DOC: Birthmark on chest covered by a large tattoo of a phoenix.

He takes a photo of the tattoo.

WORKING GIRL: Oldest livin' bird. Just keeps pullin' itself up from its own ashes. You gonna burn me?

DOC: Bit of paperwork first.

WORKING GIRL: When they dyin' they build 'emselves a nest of twigs and herbs and they sit on it waitin' for the sun to light 'em into flames. Don't struggle. Soak in the burn and out the ashes rises a new body. Rising like the sun. Towards it. Like sheddin' skin. You got tatts?

DOC: On my ankle. Exchange student in China. I asked for the Chinese symbol for faith, says wonton soup. I've grown quite attached to it over time.

iPad alert: Bling! WORKING GIRL *says what flashes up on* DOC's *iPad.*

WORKING GIRL: 'If you have good thoughts they will shine out of your face like sunbeams and you will always look lovely.' Roald Dahl.

Got these kind of facts on me Tally Ho's.

DOC: It's an app.

Was free. Recommended to me. S'posed to get me out of my own head apparently.

iPad: Bling!

Annoying. Messages keep popping up on the screen. Constantly.

WORKING GIRL: 'Life is what happens to you when you're busy making other plans'… John Lennon said that.

DOC: Might delete it.

WORKING GIRL: Get out of your own head?

DOC: It's not always a pleasant place to be.

WORKING GIRL: 17-year-old sold their kidney for an iPad. Was in the paper. True.

CELL

SON: So.
    Didn't really think about it.
    Wasn't really thinking.
    So.
    Jus' like.
    Did it.
    Had a go.
    Thwack.
    It hit.
    Crack.
    Got her.
    Right on the nut.
    Smack.
    She stop.
    Where did it come from?
    Lookin' up.
    No use lookin' there, I'm over here.
    I donno.
    Then I guess.
    I done that?
        He makes a throwing gesture.
    Smack.

MORGUE

DOC *is reading 'Ugly Mugs'.*

DOC: Worker driven to the back of Safeway. Seemed edgy. Took too long to cum. Stopped. Angry. Voice got deeper. Showed worker a knife and said he'd come back for her if she said anything.

iPad: Bling!

WORKING GIRL: Life is a journey not a destination. It's not where you're headed it's how much fun you had along the way.

DOC: Demanded money back. Stole bag. Male description: medium build, bit of stubble. Smelt strongly of cheap cologne.

iPad: Bling!

WORKING GIRL: 'The brain spends 80% of its time rewinding past events or creating perfect future scenarios.'

CELL

SON *is recalling.*

FOOTY GIRL: Did you hide it?

SON: What?

FOOTY GIRL: My bag. Keep me here longer lookin' for it? Get another shot at me.

SON: Why would I do that?

She repeats herself.

FOOTY GIRL: Cos you like me or something. Keep me here longer lookin' for it.

SON: Why would I do that?

FOOTY GIRL: Cos you like me or somethin'.

She repeats herself.

Cos you like me or somethin'

SON: No I don't. No I don't? Why I say that?

I never.

FOOTY GIRL: Woulda been clever.

SON: I never.

FOOTY GIRL: Everybody capable of anything. If they think of it. They can do it.

She repeats herself.

Everybody capable of anything. If they think of it. They can do it.

SON: Never think of doin' that.

FOOTY GIRL: No-one else about to think it.

SON: A little chunk musta fell off a star or somethin' weird.

FOOTY GIRL: But they not out.

SON: Jus' because ya can't see 'em don't mean they ain't there. A bit of meteor. God's dummy hit ya in the head. That what I said?

FOOTY GIRL: Aimed at me?

SON: Cos there's no-one else we see?

CELL

MUM *is watching* SON. *She interrupts his recall.*

MUM: Where are you?

SON: Whadda ya mean?

MUM: Where are ya?

SON: Here, where else I be?

MUM: In ya head but where'd you go?

SON: Nowhere. Here.

MUM: What you thinking there?

SON: Nothing.

MUM: Where's it takin' ya?

SON: Nowhere.

MUM: Didn't look like you here.

SON: What's that look like if I be right here in front of you but not.

MUM: I donno. What do I look like? Shadow not sharin'? I know when you here and you were gone.

SON: You think I did it?

FOOTY GIRL: Gonna give my bag back??

SON: Haven't got it.

FOOTY GIRL: You look through it?

MUM: No.

FOOTY GIRL: Who woulda taken it?

SON: Donno.

FOOTY GIRL: Why you following me?

SON: Retracing your steps.

FOOTY GIRL: Need my keys. My phone. I can't go home.

MUM: They're tellin' me ya did it.

SON: Got a tissue?

    MUM *looks for a tissue.*

FOOTY GIRL: My wallet.
SON: You're bleeding.
MUM: Had somethin' to do with it, they say.
>FOOTY GIRL *finds an apple on the ground.*
FOOTY GIRL: All's left is my apple.
MUM: Imagine. Just never comin' home.
SON: What?
MUM: The bag. That was their second clue.
SON: Can't believe…
MUM: I'd be worried sick if you never come home.
SON: I always never come home.
MUM: If I was expecting you to, I mean.
SON: How many days?
MUM: Two days they first say. But the weekend doesn't count. Your first hearing's tomorrow then they decide if ya juvenile or adult and if you can… depending on what they…
SON: No. How many days till you'd go lookin' for me.
MUM: I donno.
SON: Think about it.
MUM: Three.
SON: Three nights?
MUM: Three nights I'd start to wonder.
SON: But not worry.
MUM: After four I'd start.
SON: Four? How many if I was her?
MUM: One.
SON: One? And me four?
   After three days ya chances of being found alive are pretty grim.
MUM: That's if ya lost in the desert. A girl'd have more chance there than—
SON: Heapsa people go missin'.

MUM: Around 44,000 sexual assaults reported a year.

SON: Why you say that? Why you thinking 'bout that?

MUM: Was on me pad.

SON: What?

MUM: That lil strip ya pull off.

SON: Huh?

MUM: So the wings work. Stick.

SON: What?

MUM: All kindsa worldly info right there between me legs leakin' into me brain before I can even stick me wings down.

SON: Gross.

MUM: Ya know if a cockroach touches a human it runs away to clean itself?

That dolphins can speak? They even got names for each other.

SON: No.

MUM: Did ya know Australia got the most dangerous snake in the world? Enough venom in one bite to kill a hundred people? The most deadly fish? Just look like a flippin' rock. We got more camels here than anywhere else in the world?

SON: No.

MUM: Well, there ya go. I know.

Never bloody seen one.

Copper seems nice. The short one with the wonky eye. Seem like a nice guy. The left one. Look at the left one cos God knows what the other one's doin'. The lady. She seems bit uppity but I'm beginning to like her. Y'know the first recorded police force in Australia was made up of 12 of the most well-behaved convicts? Told me you weren't talkin'. Doin' a lot of starin' at the wall.

Beat.

The blood on the ball.

Beat.

She have a nose bleed? A little scratch on her knee?

Beat.

The bag…

SON: I never seen it.

FOOTY GIRL: You know where my key is. My phone. Wallet. You got it. Give us it.

SON: Could have. Nah, I don't really. Just teasin' ya. Maybe.

MUM: The CCTV.

SON: They say who told 'em it was me?

MUM: Was all they played on TV. Camera showed ya watchin'—

SON: Her. Told you I was.

MUM: Blockin' her path. Grabbin' her arm. She's pushin' you away.

SON: Who told them where to find me?

MUM: No trace of her.

SON: Think they know so much about me.

It show us havin' a kick?

MUM: Someone's heard a girl crying and saw someone running from the park.

SON: She wasn't crying. I didn't run.

MUM: Y'know on average a person tells four lies a day.

SON: Why you say that?

MUM: And cats have 32 muscles in each ear.

MORGUE

DOC: White station wagon. Registration RHE 3— Five foot eight. Early 40s. Mug called himself Jason. Brown eyes. Earring in left ear. He was wearing a blue tracksuit top with suit pants. A gold chain around his neck with a small 'M' on it. Worker noticed he was very clean and smelt strongly of Lynx Africa…

Mug and worker negotiated four-hour service to be completed at mug's home. Mug started out friendly and polite but became aggressive as the booking progressed. Mug deadlocked the doors detaining worker for three nights during which time he…

WORKING GIRL: Did they have a march for me? There a riot? Tools down. The big clock in town stop? Minute silence. Tears all round?

DOC: No.

WORKING GIRL: I make the news?

DOC: Umm…

WORKING GIRL: In the paper?

DOC: You don't want to read it.

> *Beat.*

Your friends had a vigil. Lots of flowers on the street.

WORKING GIRL: Shocked? When they couldn't find me? See my flowers at their feet?

DOC: Messages of sadness. Someone spray-paint R.I.P. on your corner. In a big heart. Police saw her doing it. She gave them a mouthful and they let her be.

WORKING GIRL: Jackie. Betcha. And messages?

DOC: Of sadness.

> *He continues reading 'Ugly Mugs'.*

Mug also punched worker to the face. Mug's two housemates returned. An argument broke out at which time worker was able to flee.

WORKING GIRL: So. What else they do for me?

DOC: Drove worker to beach behind BP.

WORKING GIRL: So these messages for me…
DOC: Seemed friendly.
WORKING GIRL: There many?
DOC: Ripped worker's top. Scratched her face.
WORKING GIRL: Excuse me.
DOC: Yes.
WORKING GIRL: How many there be?
DOC: Plenty.
WORKING GIRL: What they say?
DOC: People are sad.
WORKING GIRL: I'm gonna go see.

CELL / PARK

FOOTY GIRL: I'm gonna have to…

SON: What?

FOOTY GIRL: Donno.

SON: Not much of a plan.

FOOTY GIRL: Comin' up with one I am.

Try find…

SON: What?

FOOTY GIRL: Somethin' worth somethin'.

SON: Where?

FOOTY GIRL: Ask someone for somethin'. Beg.

SON: Who?

FOOTY GIRL: Rob some poor granny at an ATM.

SON: Really?

FOOTY GIRL: Sneak up behind her and snatch it.

SON: You'd do that?

FOOTY GIRL: Smash a car window. Lucky dip.

SON: You done that before?

FOOTY GIRL: That labrador. That big yellow blind donation dog. That big plastic out the front of Coles with a slit in its head for coins dog. Take it for a little walk.

SON: It's chained.

FOOTY GIRL: Steal some boltcutters from Bunnings.

SON: And probably empty.

FOOTY GIRL: And a nail gun. Hold up Macca's drive-through.

SON: How?

FOOTY GIRL: On me new bike that I cut off some pole.

SON: They don't serve you if you're not in a car.

FOOTY GIRL: Huh?

SON: Drive-through.

FOOTY GIRL: Wheel the bike into Cash Converters. Steal a car from the carpark. Break in someone's house. Fill the boot. Take—

SON: Their Xbox.

FOOTY GIRL: Their cameras and computers. With their babies' photos on them. The only ones they took. They'll put up some huge reward.

SON: Or PS4 might get ya more.

FOOTY GIRL: I'll just say I found 'em.

SON: We'll steal their dogs too.

FOOTY GIRL: Bit suss I do both. And I'm not lookin' after no dogs till they pay.

SON: The fountain. Where everyone chucks in coins and makes a wish. We'll go there.

FOOTY GIRL: Bad luck that. To steal wish money. Anyway there's never many gold ones. And the water's cold as fuck.

SON: We'll take the silver to the pokies. Double it.

FOOTY GIRL: It's wish money. You'll double your bad luck.

SON: What's so great 'bout wishes?

FOOTY GIRL: The hope in 'em. Ya don't mess with other people's hope. Sacred. Ya don't know what they wished for. Or why. Could be anything. You can kiss me.

SON: They mighta wished… Kiss you?

You wanna kiss me?

FOOTY GIRL: If it gets rid of that stupid look on your face. Do you wish I'd kiss you?

SON: You wanna do that?

FOOTY GIRL: For my bag. Kill two wishes with one stone or whatever.

SON: You'd kiss me?

FOOTY GIRL: You know where it is, don't ya? Cos you never said no. Should be thankful.

SON: Why?

FOOTY GIRL: Compliment.

SON: Why's that?

FOOTY GIRL: Means I don't think you're too ugly. To go through with it. I won't spew. Should be happy. Does it?

SON: What?

FOOTY GIRL: Make you happy?

SON: Happy you won't spew?

FOOTY GIRL: Hard to crack, aren't ya?

Beat.

Maybe I just punch up a bank teller.

All in the bag and I won't stab ya.

SON: I'm not that hard to crack. You'd do it with a knife?

FOOTY GIRL: All in the bag and I'll let ya keep ya life.

SON: Really? A knife not a gun? You'd cut someone?

FOOTY GIRL: Nah. Set fire to their face then run like fuck.

SON: Harsh.

FOOTY GIRL: Chuck acid in their eyes. Run so far I get burning vomit throat.

SON: And stomach stitches. Have you ever run that hard?

FOOTY GIRL: Run so far I'm old by the time I get there.

SON: No-one recognise you then.

I wouldn't spew neither.

FOOTY GIRL: You're so weird.

MORGUE

DOC: Mug went into servo and was seen making a phone call. Mug returned and offered worker some Savoury Shapes. Kept asking worker if she could 'see the flavour'. He was complaining it said on the packet 'with flavour you can see' and could worker see any? Worker replied that she thought she could. He seemed very agitated about this. Seriously?

WORKING GIRL: *You were the funniest psycho I ever did have the pleasure to adore. Heaven just got interesting. Love, Brian.*

There's a whole wall of 'em.

DOC: Told you.

WORKING GIRL: Nah ya didn't. Whole wall of—

DOC: Sadness. Mug complained of having a bad day and that he was good with explosives and was going to blow up an Arnott's factory.

WORKING GIRL: Flowers and all.

DOC: I know. Whole wall.

Offered worker $200 anal no condom. Worker declined. Mug said he would double it if he could defecate in her mouth. Worker declined.

WORKING GIRL: What you lookin' for?

DOC: Not sure. Mug grabbed her by the hair and dragged her out of the car.

WORKING GIRL: *I will always remember your kindness to me as I summon your smile before I sleep.*

DOC: Mug drove off with worker's belongings.

WORKING GIRL: Thanks Nigel.

DOC: Mug stated his name was Dave. Anglo. Five foot ten. Said he'd go to ATM after service. Worker declined. Mug locked doors.

WORKING GIRL: *What for is my heart's treasure no more? You were my favourite hoar.* Spelt h.o.a.r. Written on the back of a Carlton Draught beer coaster with a daffodil. *Love, Mark.* Mark?

DOC: Mug became verbally aggressive accusing worker of trying to rip him off stating… Oh, geez.

Stating he deserved a discount and that he could get it off one of his daughters for free.

WORKING GIRL: *To the lady in the long black boots. I'm goin' to look for you in rainbows.* From the little girl lived in the flat below me. A drawing of a rainbow and me. Sittin' on top with my boots on, with her cat got run over 'bout a month ago. She's a really weirdo kid. Real starer. I stare back. Lil turd sittin' on the step. Stare stare stare. We made friends right there. Even when her parents callin' her she rather stay talk to me.

DOC: He also bragged about sitting in his car outside the school gates before and after school masturbating as he watched children enter and exit. Worker said she was uncomfortable with conversation. Mug slapped worker across the face and pushed her out of the vehicle. Leaving her to find her own way back.

WORKING GIRL: You should see Jackie's note says '*gonna miss ya askin'*' and she's sticky-taped one of her rollies to it with a match and the striker off the side of her matchbox. And stapled a photocopy, like she wouldn't part with the original, of the two of us hangin' out front of the souvlaki van used to be on the corner, years back. Crack me up. Takin' a break. Hidin' from cops. Both us look off our chops. Arms wrapped round each other. Jack looks like she borrowed her hair from Bon Jovi and mine looks like it's had a Tina Turner attack. Like we're their biggest fans. And then it says 'LOVED' underneath in big thick Texta.

DOC: Offered worker Mogodon. Bit of stubble. Silver diamond earring left ear. Smelt strongly of cheap cologne. Bit of stubble. Silver diamond earring. Left ear. Smelt strongly of cheap cologne.

    DOC *flicks back a couple of pages.*

WORKING GIRL: You onto something? How ya goin' there in ya own head?

DOC: Lynx Africa?

WORKING GIRL: *Mum asked me to bring down some flowers. She's not doin' too good. Took me hours to get here and it's done my head in thinkin' of what to write. Say it right. Nearly turned back. Didn't think I could do it. But I didn't want to fuck this up too. If there's any way you can read this, sorry. You'll always be my sister. I'll always regret what I said. Always. Keep thinkin' of the time I told you I needed to get out of town. You drove me to the frickin' desert. Broome. Fuck sake. Mooned all the buses along the way. Kept us awake laughing. Distract us from all that road kill. Can still see you now. Laughin' so hard ya can't breathe. You always went the full mile. So gutted ya had to leave. Always remember your smile. Kiss Kiss. Mum and sis.*

Silence.

A couple and their dog were standing there reading some while I got stuck on that one. Not many girls around? Streets a frickin' ghost town

Did you say Lynx Africa? I saw you write that down.

PARK

FOOTY GIRL: I don't want it back.

SON: What?

FOOTY GIRL: Bag.

SON: Wait. Yes you do.

FOOTY GIRL: Nah don't.

SON: You must.

FOOTY GIRL: Feels better without it actually. Lighter.

SON: You need it.

FOOTY GIRL: Nah don't. Have everything.

SON: Your ID.

FOOTY GIRL: Have all of me.

SON: Your key.

FOOTY GIRL: Get another one cut.

SON: Ya phone?

FOOTY GIRL: Never rings

SON: What about ya wallet?

FOOTY GIRL: Nothin' really in it.

SON: Look like you about to cry.

FOOTY GIRL: Bit of meteor. God's dummy in my eye.

SON: Don't.

FOOTY GIRL: Not. Why would I?

SON: Don't like you sad.

FOOTY GIRL: Not. I'm glad.

SON: Glad?

FOOTY GIRL: Still got my apple.

SON: Glad, is it? On your face?

FOOTY GIRL: No reason this look hasn't got one.

SON: Gone somewhere.

FOOTY GIRL: I'm nowhere.

SON: You're somewhere.

FOOTY GIRL: Can't think where.

SON: But you there. Glad? Where you are?

FOOTY GIRL: Tired.

SON: Of?

FOOTY GIRL: It all. Sick of.

MORGUE

DOC: Dilated pupils.

>   *He extracts a leaf from* WORKING GIRL*'s hair.*

Debris. A young leaf off an old tree.

Caesarean scar.

Expel the bowel.

WORKING GIRL: Your job's foul.

DOC: What do you think?

WORKING GIRL: What?

DOC: Happened?

WORKING GIRL: Gets blurry. Whack and blackout.

From behind? Grabbed?

DOC: Have to cut your nails. See if we can find him there.

WORKING GIRL: In different skin everywhere.

Tied up an' whacked over the head with somethin' blunt. Was I that?

DOC: Hope for residue. A sample of brain tissue. Pulmonary vein for the chemical analysis and your stomach contents. Get a time on it. And the PSA.

WORKING GIRL: Hey?

DOC: DNA testing. More accurate findings in vaginal decay.

WORKING GIRL: No way.

DOC: A few moistened swabs on the dried stains. Look for hair and fibres. Every contact leaves a trace.

WORKING GIRL: I know. Look at my face.

DOC: Capture his biological signature.

WORKING GIRL: Smash any teeth out?

DOC: What teeth you had you somehow managed to keep.

WORKING GIRL: My lips take a punch? Is that the swell? Eyes gouged?

DOC: No. Framed in a bruise.

WORKING GIRL: Gravel rash on my chin.

DOC: Blisters on the feet.

WORKING GIRL: Dragged along concrete?

DOC: Compressed trachea.

WORKING GIRL: Hair wrenched from the skull?

DOC: Yes.

WORKING GIRL: Ow.

DOC: Fractured hyoid. Would of resulted in the frightening sensation of air hunger. Blood in the cavity of nose.

Scratches on your scars.

WORKING GIRL: Buried alive somewhere. Was I? Screamin' up dirt?

DOC: You were found. You're here.

WORKING GIRL: Oh yeah. Not even hidden?

DOC: By a girl walking a dog.

WORKING GIRL: She found me?

DOC: Out earnin' her pocket money.

WORKING GIRL: Back roads? Laneway?

DOC: Park. Ditch.

Weight. 47 kilos.

WORKING GIRL: Air hunger you say?

DOC: Strangulation. 7 to 14 seconds. A minute at the most if they fumbled. Passed away a few minutes later. If they knew what they were doing. If they knew what they were doing.

He puts on a splash-proof apron, preparing for the autopsy.

WORKING GIRL: What's that for?

DOC: The big Y…

WORKING GIRL: Why?

DOC: From each of your shoulders down the middle of your chest and finishing at your sternum.

WORKING GIRL: Why?

DOC: Access.

WORKING GIRL: What?

DOC: All of you. The big Y.

WORKING GIRL: I don't get a say?

DOC: Don't really work that way.

WORKING GIRL: You think you'll find him there? In me?

DOC: Worth a look.

WORKING GIRL: How you gonna do that?

DOC: Saw through the ribs. Scissors to snip the attachment tissue.

WORKING GIRL: How you gonna cut round me feelings?

DOC: They should have taken leave.

WORKING GIRL: Ya gonna put it all back? In its place?

DOC: Most of it. In a plastic bag.

WORKING GIRL: Plastic bag? Most of it?

DOC: Most goes back in the bag. Prevents leakage.

WORKING GIRL: Ya gonna shove most the leftover mangled bits back into me in a plastic bag?

DOC: Not shove.

WORKING GIRL: I don't think my feelings have taken leave.

DOC: Autopsia. 'To see for oneself.' First done to animals. Some used to believe the intestines and liver contained messages from divine spirits. Clues to predict the future.

WORKING GIRL: You ever find them?

DOC: Feelings?

WORKING GIRL: The mugs. In me. Apparently.

DOC: Sometimes.

WORKING GIRL: Sometimes you get clues to predict the future. This must be part of the burn. Before I rise.

Excuse me. How are you going to deal with my eyes?

PARK

FOOTY GIRL: Just let me get one look at it. My phone. Get one number.

SON: Tell me why you can't go home?

Okay. If you can hit the bin with ya apple. I'll do one of the things like steal the car. Whatever. The labrador. You miss I get to make one wish and you have to do it.

FOOTY GIRL: I'll go to the cops tell 'em you've got it.

SON: Got what? Info about that smashed light?

FOOTY GIRL: Reckon they find the gash on my head more interesting. Might wanna know where that come from.

SON: Handcuff the sky. Take it in for questioning. You got nothin'. They just send you home.

FOOTY GIRL: My boyfriend will sort it out.

SON: You don't got one. Do ya?

FOOTY GIRL: He's coming here straight after his martial art class.

SON: Oh yeah, what kinda martial arts?

FOOTY GIRL: He's huge. He's the teacher. Kung fu. Yeah Sifu. Paul.

SON: What time's he finish?

FOOTY GIRL: Should be here any second.

SON: I'll wait with you till he gets here.

FOOTY GIRL: Gimme my bag, I call him. Tell him exactly where we are.

SON: Nobody comin'.

FOOTY GIRL: He's been teaching me. I can snap someone's neck with just one jab.

SON: Show us some moves.

FOOTY GIRL: It's against the code to show off.

SON: You're full of shit.

FOOTY GIRL: Watch it if I was you. Might feel the need to defend myself. One smack crack ya head open.

SON: Oh yeah. Have a throw. Ya never know.

FOOTY GIRL: We both do. I miss. I owe.
SON: But what you don't know. If you hit. I'll give you … somethin'.
FOOTY GIRL: What?
SON: Somethin' worth somethin'.
FOOTY GIRL: You ain't got nothin' worth somethin'.
SON: A wish.
FOOTY GIRL: My bag.
SON: And ya can't say it out loud or it won't come true.
FOOTY GIRL: Then how you know what I want?
SON: And it's serious. No backin' out. You have to do it.
FOOTY GIRL: So do you.
SON: Scared?
FOOTY GIRL: Of?
SON: Losin'.
FOOTY GIRL: Nah.
SON: It's like a promise ya have to keep.
FOOTY GIRL: You do too.
SON: And you have to be blindfolded else it's too easy.
FOOTY GIRL: Get real.
SON: That's the deal.
FOOTY GIRL: A wish. You said I get a wish.

He blindfolds her.

SON: A wish. You get a wish too.
FOOTY GIRL: You know what I want.

He spins her around in circles.

SON: And they're full of hope. Wouldn't mess with other people's hope. Sacred. Ya never know what they wish for or why. Could be anything.

He faces her towards himself. She tosses an apple. He catches it.

Missed.

He sits back in the cell chair…

CELL

SON *is holding the apple.*

SON: I just wanted one.

MUM: You gonna eat it or save it?

SON: What type is it?

MUM: Royal cocky. Yeah. Up there on its throne all crowned up.

MUG: Stinks. Smell it. Slut scent.

MUM: No, galah. That's right. A royal galah. A princely one right there. A shiny red Harry. I thought. The best. Ya just gonna stare at it?

SON: Where did you get it?

MUG: Out on the street like hard rubbish.

MUM: Shops.

SON: Thanks.

MUM: What ya asked for, isn't it?

SON: Yep.

MUM: Could of bought more.

SON: Only wanted the one.

MUG: Mangy dogs.

MUM: But ya said that.

SON: It's exactly what I wanted.

MUM: I know. Was hard to choose the right one. Didn't want one that when ya bit into was all rotten an' alien-lookin'. Bugs ya never coulda imagine the ugliness of, jumpin' into ya mouth and I donno, takin' over ya insides. All cos my hand land on the wrong one. Much easier buyin' a few and takin' care with the first bite.

SON: Reckon I can survive an apple.

MUM: Good to have a backup though. So all the hopes don't lie with the one.

SON: It's perfect. In the paper? The things they say.

MUM: Thought they wouldn't let ya read it.

SON: Says friendless liar and jealous stalker with mental problems and a mum that don't wanna know me. It said all that. About me.

MUM: Scum of the earth.

SON: My face blurred out but if you squinted your eyes.

MUM: Makin' us all out like monsters.

SON: Is that what you said? I'm mental and ya don't wanna know me?

MUM: Whadda you think? Here, aren't I?

SON: You think I'm a liar?

MUM: Never spoke to no-one.

You see what they say about me?

SON: A bit unkempt. Appeared drunk and you swore at the man taking your photo.

MUM: One drink with me dinner. He knocks at the door. Piss off. In me face.

Gawkin'.

Chewin' on our business.

Our names fat in their mouth.

In their spit.

She's the one.

Her son.

The quiet one. Toxic womb she got.

Must have.

Brought it up to slay us all.

Not one of us. Her. That one and her son.

Musta done somethin' to it.

Dropped it on its head. Never fed it proper or played with it long enough. Read it the wrong book. Abused it.

Made it cry for fun. Left it to fend for itself.

Let the world get to it.

What did she expect?

Let it drink tap water.

At least one molecule of H₂O in every glass has once passed through a dinosaur. Fact.

SON: You brought me an apple. I'm happy.

MUM: No air in here. Smells like mould.
Gotta move the car. One more fine and I'll have to sell an organ. And it won't be mine.

MUM *exits.*

FOOTY GIRL: Did you like it?

SON: What?

FOOTY GIRL: Having it sucked.

SON: Was alright.

FOOTY GIRL: You're so weird.
Got your wish.
S'posed to like it.
You had it done before?

SON: Was good.

FOOTY GIRL: Haven't, have ya?

SON: What?

FOOTY GIRL: Had it done before.

SON: Yes I have. Heaps.

FOOTY GIRL: Ya don't have to like it if you don't wanna.

SON: Liked it.

FOOTY GIRL: You gonna give it over then?

SON: Huh?

FOOTY GIRL: You're half the deal.

SON: You missed. That was the deal. A wish if ya hit but you didn't.

FOOTY GIRL: You didn't say you were going to twirl me round in circles too.

SON: Blindfold. Everyone knows that's what ya do.

FOOTY GIRL: Just give my bag back.

SON: I don't have it.

FOOTY GIRL: Liar.

SON: I'll help you look for it.

FOOTY GIRL: Bastard. Prick fuck. I've looked.

SON: This whole park we haven't.

FOOTY GIRL: Why don't you just give it back?

SON: I never said I had it.

FOOTY GIRL: Never said you didn't.

SON: I wanted you to kiss me then.

FOOTY GIRL: You're fucked.

SON: We'll find it.

FOOTY GIRL: Why you playing games with me?

SON: I'm not. Let's look.

FOOTY GIRL: Where haven't I?

SON: Way over there. Somewhere out of sight. Them bushes. That's where I'd throw it.

FOOTY GIRL: Why would you steal a bag then throw it?

SON: Take the good shit. Piff it.

FOOTY GIRL: Then if it's there it's empty.

SON: Let's look. Come.

>   FOOTY GIRL *doesn't.*

Fine. I'll look.

PARK

SON, *standing frozen. Watching. Witnessing an assault of* WORKING GIRL. MUG *appears out of the shadows.*

MUG: What are you lookin' at?

SON: Sorry, didn't see you there.

MUG: See what?

SON: What?

MUG: What you see?

SON: Nothin'.

MUG: Why you sorry?

SON: Interrupting.

MUG: What?

SON: Donno.

MUG: Sorry for interrupting what ya donno? Must of seen something. Did you?

SON: Nothin'. Didn't see nothin'.

MUG: Hear something?

SON: Not really.

MUG: Not really isn't nothin' but, is it?

SON: Nothin'. I didn't hear her.

MUG: Her? Did you? That somethin'? Were just playing a little game.

SON: Are ya?

MUG: She's alright.

SON: Oh right.

MUG: Out on the corner. Loose. This is what we're up against. What are we supposed to do?

SON: Who?

MUG: Smell that?

SON: What?

MUG: That smell. Stinks. Smell it.
That smell of me getting away with it. Delicious. Smell it?

SON: What you talkin' 'bout?

MUG: Smell it. See?

SON: Not really.

MUG: Doing everyone a favour.

SON: Didn't see ya. Didn't even hear ya doin' what ya…

MUG: What? What I doing? What?

SON: Strangle. Dick spitting, hair flying. Choke. Punch and the scream. Is that you mean? Cos I never seen it.

MUG: Just doing a little shoplifting.

SON: I was just cutting through.

MUG: Bit of break and enter is all.

SON: Better get back.

MUG: Little five-finger discount.

SON: Wasn't even watching where I was going.

MUG: Hear the scream?

SON: Whose?

MUG: That's the way. Good to have ya on the team.

    MUG *pats* SON *on the back.*

SON: [*to himself*] Her blood on me.

MUG: Good shot, was it not? The punch. Shut the thing up. You hear the scream stop.

SON: Pop. I woulda heard the crunch. Watched her drop.

MUG: So ya saw?

SON: If I hadn't been lookin' the other way would I have?

MUG: That doubt in the eye. Pleading. One of the closest friends I have. That bit of me they see make them look at me that way.

SON: Didn't want him to see the doubt in me eye. The pleadin'. Didn't want him to see his closest friend in me.

    MUM *enters, overhears* SON *seemingly talking to himself.*

MUM: What?
SON: It's a song.
MUG: No-one watchin'.
SON: Nup.
MUG: No-one sayin' nothin'. Right?
MUM: Ya just gonna mumble it?
SON: Better get goin'.
MUG: Don't wanna play?
SON: My girlfriend's waiting.
MUG: You get what I'm sayin', don't ya?
SON: What?
MUM: You okay?
MUG: In this together. Doing our bit. Out on the street.
MUM: Who cares what people say.
MUG: Face all made-up. Invite smudged all over the lips.
MUM: They can go to hell.
MUG: Glossed. Lubed an' boobed an' hair tossed. Slut salads.
MUM: But ya gotta tell me.
MUG: Hard rubbish. Pieces of worthless.
MUM: What do you think?
MUG: Scraps of nothin'.
MUM: You gone to that place where you go?
MUG: Trashin' up the joint.
MUM: Trust me.
MUG: Someone's gotta be the ranger.
MUM: You can tell me.
MUG: Mangy dogs.
SON: I committed silence. I'm on the team. It's my fault.
MUM: What?
SON: You think I'm a beast?

MUM: No. They say you might have been provoked into behaving like one.

SON: How?

MUM: Mosquitoes are attracted to people who recently ate a banana.

SON: Huh?

MUM: What was she wearing?

SON: Why?

MUM: Self-defence. Maybe there's a way through there.

SON: Way through?

MUM: Building your case, they are. She dress dangerously?

SON: Whadda ya mean?

MUM: Provoke ya?

SON: How?

MUM: Y'know dress too high, top too low? Hypnotising ya with what might be available?

SON: She had tracksuit pants on.

MUM: I know it don't sound right but was she invitin' it? Were they tight?

SON: No.

MUM: Slung low?

SON: I donno.

MUM: Showin' off her y'know.

SON: What?

MUM: Camel toe.

SON: Stop it. Gross. No.

MUM: Skimpy top fallin' off her shoulder?

SON: T-shirt.

MUM: Show her shape?

SON: Clothes don't ask for a fight.

MUM: There a fight?

SON: You're confusing me. I wouldn't do that. No matter what she wear.

MUM: I'm just tryna get to the facts.

SON: We were going to set fire to someone's face.

MUM: Don't be smart.

SON: Chuck acid in their eyes.

MUM: Whose?

SON: Bank tellers.

MUM: What are you talking about?

SON: Everybody capable of anything. If they think of it they can do it.

MUM: You were thinkin' of that?

You were gonna do that?

SON: You're so weird.

MUM: I'm not the one sittin' in some mouldy cell talkin' about settin' fire to someone's face. Oh yes I am. And whose fault's that? Oh hang on. That's right. I can go.

SON: No.

MUM: Ya finished bein' smart?

SON: Sorry.

MUM: It was gettin' late, you said the moon was out.

SON: And the sun. They were sorta passing each other on their shift.

MUM: Everyone knows it's not safe in the dark. Alone. Outta sight.

SON: We were right.

MUM: Anyone coulda been about. On anything. Who knows in what mind.

Gettin' into a bit of a scrag over the ball.

SON: Jus' muckin' round.

MUM: See. That's probably all it was. This is good. Probably how you got the blood on your shirt. Accidents happen. Four people a year die just trying to put their pants on. 150 from falling coconuts. Random. Out of the sky. Wrong place, wrong time. Sorry. No-one's fault. Not the coconuts'. Or the tree it fell from's. Ya just gotta find the courage and say.

SON: My fingerprints everywhere.

MUM: Shut up about that. Of course they are. Ya spent half the week there.

The parkin' here's shit.

Gotta go move the wheels. Check for chalk.

SON: I know ya go out to smoke.

MUM: No I don't.

SON: Can smell it. Stinks.

MUM: I've given up.

SON: Y'know on average a person tells four lies a day. Three left.

MUM: I've cut back.

SON: Two.

MUM: I've only had a few.

SON: One.

MUM: I'm the mum. Not killin' no-one.

SON: None.

MUM: And you're past smart-arse. They'll take that into account.

SON: Why?

MUM: See if you're a fair player.

PARK

SON *coming back from witnessing the assault.*

SON: Come with me.
    He grabs FOOTY GIRL*'s arm.*
FOOTY GIRL: What are ya doin'?
SON: Come.
FOOTY GIRL: My bag.
SON: Come this way.
FOOTY GIRL: Said you'd find it.
SON: It's gone. Not there. Someone's taken it.
FOOTY GIRL: How you know?
SON: It's not there. I've looked. Come.
FOOTY GIRL: Wait.
SON: Come.
FOOTY GIRL: Why are you being such a suck?
SON: Fuck. Just do as I say.
    FOOTY GIRL *walks off.*
  Where you goin'?
FOOTY GIRL: Don't speak to me that way.
SON: Don't just walk off.
FOOTY GIRL: Stop thinkin' you can tell me what to do.
SON: Please.
FOOTY GIRL: Why?
SON: You got nowhere to go.
FOOTY GIRL: So.
SON: It's got too dark.
FOOTY GIRL: I'll walk in the light.
SON: I'll walk with you.
FOOTY GIRL: Don't need you to.

SON: Make sure you get where ya goin'.
FOOTY GIRL: I'm right.
SON: Don't care if we walk all night.
FOOTY GIRL: You're not invited.
SON: Safer to be with me.
FOOTY GIRL: We'll see.
SON: Will I see ya again?
FOOTY GIRL: Hope not.
SON: Stop. You don't mean that.
FOOTY GIRL: Just because you don't mean what you say don't mean I don't.
SON: I never said I had it.
FOOTY GIRL: Whatever.
SON: Just tell us where ya gonna go?
FOOTY GIRL: That car.
SON: Why?
FOOTY GIRL: Ask for a lift.
SON: Where?
FOOTY GIRL: Why you care?
SON: Won't get far.
FOOTY GIRL: Huh?
SON: No-one even in that car.
FOOTY GIRL: The next one that comes along.
SON: You're just bein' stupid.
FOOTY GIRL: Maybe taxi.
SON: You got no money.
FOOTY GIRL: Exactly. If they don't do it they'll call a mate who will. Job swap.
SON: What?
FOOTY GIRL: You heard.

SON: Job swap? What you mean?

FOOTY GIRL: What do you reckon?

Beat.

SON: You can't drive a taxi.

FOOTY GIRL: Use the driver's dick as a gear stick to get it wherever I want it to go.

SON: That's crap. Who told you that?

FOOTY GIRL: Just good to be aware of your options. What?

SON: What?

FOOTY GIRL: That look on your face.

SON: What look?

FOOTY GIRL: You-think-I'm-a-slut look.

SON: You'd do that?

FOOTY GIRL: Why not? My cousin does. But she doesn't tell anyone. Is that a yes?

SON: No. Why doesn't she tell anyone?

FOOTY GIRL: Donno. Maybe they pull that face you got on.

SON: What if something? Someone does?

FOOTY GIRL: What?

SON: I donno.

FOOTY GIRL: Sky might fall down, freak. Nothin' gonna happen.

SON: Unless someone decides to make it.

Bad stuff happens everywhere.

FOOTY GIRL: So does good stuff. Besides, everyone does it. May as well make some money from it while it's happening.

SON: Don't think you should.

FOOTY GIRL: Why?

SON: Sell your body.

FOOTY GIRL: Not. Need it. I'm doing sex, not body parts.

SON: You know what I mean.

FOOTY GIRL: No.
SON: Against the law. Dangerous.
FOOTY GIRL: You are one of them.
SON: You're not a pro.
FOOTY GIRL: Who says 'pro'? And how you know?
SON: You fumbled a bit. Prostitute.
FOOTY GIRL: Your dodgy zip. Don't say that. It's sex worker.
SON: Doesn't suit you.
FOOTY GIRL: Doesn't suit who?
SON: You shouldn't go. Alone. Don't.
FOOTY GIRL: Goin'.
SON: Let's keep lookin' for your bag.
FOOTY GIRL: There's not enough in it even if I found it.
SON: I'll look after the dogs.
FOOTY GIRL: Huh?
SON: Ransom money.
FOOTY GIRL: So weird.
SON: Why?
FOOTY GIRL: You.
SON: Our car.

    FOOTY GIRL *starts to leave.*

You can stay at mine.
FOOTY GIRL: I'm fine.
SON: But you're not even very good at it.
FOOTY GIRL: You didn't complain.
SON: In too much pain. Was bad. Worst I ever had.
FOOTY GIRL: Didn't look that way to me.
SON: You couldn't give that away for free.
FOOTY GIRL: You're mental.
SON: Who'd want you? Not even gentle. All gulp an' teeth. No rhythm.

FOOTY GIRL: You were frozen stiff.

SON: And a bit… ugly. Who gonna pay for ugly? Are you really goin'?

FOOTY GIRL: Cold.

SON: Don't.

FOOTY GIRL: What?

SON: Stay. Don't go. Ya don't know what ya doin'.

FOOTY GIRL: Yes I do. Suckin' someone off for heapsa cash.

SON: But what if /

FOOTY GIRL: / Someone nice. Kind. Handsome gentleman with a good sense of humour.

SON: Fat fuck'll have breath like tuna.

FOOTY GIRL: He'll probably take me to his holiday house.

SON: They stink.

FOOTY GIRL: Who?

SON: Slut scent.

FOOTY GIRL: What?

SON: Invite smudged all over the lips. Trash. Hard rubbish. Pieces of worthless nothings. Mangy dogs.

FOOTY GIRL: What are you even saying?

SON: You're not goin' nowhere.

> SON *blocks* FOOTY GIRL.

FOOTY GIRL: Says who?

SON: I know where ya bag is.

> SON *pulls* FOOTY GIRL*'s arm*

FOOTY GIRL: So what? Don't. Let go. Don't be psycho.

SON: I seen it. Just before. A guy behind that tree.

FOOTY GIRL: You don't own me.

SON: Smashin' this chick. Getting' a freebie.

> *He grabs at* FOOTY GIRL *again. There is a struggle that is caught on CCTV.*

FOOTY GIRL: Don't. Leave me. Goin' ta go see which way that four-wheel drive's heading.

SON: All over her.

FOOTY GIRL: He's watching.

SON: Listen.

FOOTY GIRL: Let go.

SON: Doubt in your eye.

He steps in front of her.

FOOTY GIRL: All I gotta do is scream.

SON: Don't be a bitch.

FOOTY GIRL: See ya.

She walks toward the car.

SON: Slut salad.

FOOTY GIRL: I'm askin' for a lift, ya fuckstick.

SON: Stop. Now. Pause. Enough.

FOOTY GIRL: What?

SON: Don't go any further. We're gonna rewind. You're as good a player as me. Sorry. Shoulda let you be.

FOOTY GIRL: Not somethin' ya said. In ya head.

SON: Stuck there.

I'm gonna think it that way.

Think you back. Say it.

FOOTY GIRL: Enough.

SON: Thinking it. Boom onto my chest. Go.

FOOTY GIRL: No.

SON: You say you got sisters. Ask me.

FOOTY GIRL: You got sisters?

Gonna give it back?

Need my key.

Did you like it?

You're weird.

Still got my apple.

SON: What are you doing?

FOOTY GIRL: I'm fast-forwarding.

It's wish money.

Ya don't mess with other people's hope.

So weird.

You didn't complain.

Don't be psycho.

All I gotta do is scream.

SON: But you're making me skip over bits.

FOOTY GIRL: I'm getting to the end where I say goodbye.

SON: Why?

FOOTY GIRL: I have to go.

SON: No.

FOOTY GIRL: That's when you feel me most.

SON: Don't.

You can kiss me. Go to there?

FOOTY GIRL: You'll get stuck. Trap us there.

SON: No I won't.

FOOTY GIRL: How many times have I undone your dodgy zip?

SON: Sorry.

FOOTY GIRL: Just tell 'em all you know so I can go.

SON: She has two eyes not three. Boom. Onto my chest. Thought it was never gonna land. Like it was gonna bounce back off the sun. Every little move she made.

FOOTY GIRL: Ugly slut salad? Invite smudged all over my mangy dog lips? They found my bag. Near a body. Near a blanket.

SON: Stop it.

FOOTY GIRL: A bloodied rock in the dirt. The blood on your shirt. They think you did the light too. CCTV looked bit ugly.

SON: Wasn't me. Black four-wheel drive. Didn't see his face. Just a shadow.

FOOTY GIRL: My stomach was makin' growling sounds. Felt a little bit queasy cos I hadn't eaten much and I didn't realise how dry I was. My lips kept sticking together.

SON: Couldn't unstick my eyes.

The sound of car doors locking.

FOOTY GIRL: 'Who would you choose to be if you could be anyone?' He ask.

Me was alright. 'Me. How about you?' He never answer. 'You seem alright too', I say. He glance away.

SON: She never even look back to see them stuck.

FOOTY GIRL: My favourite song came on the radio. A sign. Things were gonna go alright. Seats were really warm. Scratches all up my side of the upholstery. Interior door…

SON: Over and over all I saw.

FOOTY GIRL: Must have a dog. Cute lil puppy with sharp claws. A cap. Carnival across the front. Remember cos at first I thought it said carnivore.

SON: Got in. She's smiling.

FOOTY GIRL: He smoked. Car smelt like spray. He offered me some whisky when I said I didn't smoke. Offered him a bite of me apple. No thanks. Okay. Didn't really want ya slobber on it anyway. Saw a packet on the dash. Couldn't see all the letters cos it's half under somethin'. Hidden. Said somethin' 'adon'. Short for Adonis. God of beauty and desire. Adonis but without the 'is'. Packet said something 'ADON'.

She takes a bite of her apple.

SON: Bright as day in the moonlight.

Over and over and over. She's smiling. Beautiful.

Will I see you again?

FOOTY GIRL: Hope not.

FOOTY GIRL *leaves.*

SON: Stop.
You don't mean that.
He is alone.
Just cos you don't mean what you say don't mean I don't.

MORGUE

The morgue table is now empty. DOC *is talking to the photos he has been taking of* WORKING GIRL *throughout. The photos are brutal. Showing the injuries she would have sustained. He lets each one drop onto the morgue table throughout his last speech.*

DOC: You didn't eat lunch or dinner. A piece of toast with Vegemite, a fried dim sim and a bite of a Mars bar to soak up the bourbon, bupranorphine and Mogodon. Must've slipped it to you in the swig of whisky. Found traces of Lynx Africa in your skin samples. Consistent with what was under your nails and also some fragments of leather. Upholstery from the car. They're trying to trace the model. Well done there. We're building a profile. So we may clean up if all the stars align. You did good.

You're all tucked up with cotton wool now. I took special care with your stitching. Your tattoos all intact. Tried to cut round your feelings. Hope I managed. I clipped a wing but it's back where it was. You're ready.

iPad: Bling!

'Life isn't about waiting for the storm to pass it's about learning to dance in the rain.'

Don't struggle. Soak in the burn and out of the ashes rises a new body.

CELL

MUM: All the elements of the human body can be found in dust. Shouldna read that one before walkin' into ya room. Streamin' up into the light it was. Dust. Dead skin, decay, meteorites and dust-mite shit. That's what dust is. Got a gobful as I opened your curtain and let in the sun. Dust. Streaming up into it. Gave ya doona a good shake. Dust. Washed ya covers. Dust. And I donno… missed ya. Replaced the broken slat on your bed. And filled that hole in your wall with plaster stuff. And it must of been my lucky day because they didn't even charge me for it. Practically ran through the carpark to my car before they spotted it sittin' on the bottom of the trolley. Looks a bit crap. But it's fixed. And we can paint over it. Freshen up. While I wait. We wait. Every single person has a unique tongue print. No two tongues are the same. And we'll see.

Lights out.

THE END

GRIFFIN THEATRE
COMPANY AND
MALTHOUSE THEATRE
PRESENT THE WORLD
PREMIERE OF

UGLY MUGS
BY PETA BRADY

Director Marion Potts
Designer Michael Hankin
Lighting Designer Lucy Birkinshaw
Composer Darrin Verhagen
With Harry Borland, Peta Brady, Steven Le Marquand and Sara West

GRIFFIN THEATRE COMPANY
SBW STABLES THEATRE
18 JULY – 23 AUGUST

Co-produced with

Government Partners

PLAYWRIGHT'S NOTE
A STORY OF THE STREET

Street-based sex work is illegal in Victoria. This anomaly in the law creates barriers between police and street-based sex workers, who are hence less likely to report violent clients (known as 'mugs'). It strips street-based sex workers of the legal rights that others, in different occupations, take for granted, and leaves the community more vulnerable.

'Ugly Mugs' is a grassroots pamphlet developed by the Prostitute Collective of Victoria (now RHED) in 1986. It was created as a response to the under-reporting of violent incidents committed against sex workers and the lack of support and protection they receive from police and legal institutions. My play *Ugly Mugs* is a look at the persistent vulnerability of women to violence on the street. (While not all sex workers are women, the majority of violent acts described in the pamphlet are against women.)

None of the 'Ugly Mugs' reports used in my play are anyone's direct experience. I have stayed very close to the territory they contain without being specific enough as to be identifiable. The only non-fiction within my fiction has been obtained with consent. Thank you to those that have contributed to this piece along the way. I have badgered many a friend, colleague, client, cast member and stranger. You have provided me with content and dramaturgy for which I am forever grateful.

Special thanks to Marion Potts for taking a chance on this one: for commissioning the work and her ongoing support throughout the entire process. I'm feelin' the privilege. And to Lee Lewis at Griffin Theatre Company for also taking a risk on this new work: programming it and being so encouraging.

This story is inspired by those who endure violence on the street and at worst, those who have lost their lives. It is not about any one person. It is unfortunately the story of many.

Peta Brady

DIRECTOR'S NOTE

Ugly Mugs began when Peta Brady came to the theatre in early 2012 to tell myself and our Associate Writer Van Badham about what she'd been working on. She pulled an 'Ugly Mugs' pamphlet out of a thick file of research material and we were immediately transfixed. Horrified, moved, confronted by our own ignorance, this was documentation that pinpointed the brutality of the streets we drive through every day. It exposed a woeful tendency to hide our heads in the sand – a kind of collective collusion that we felt compelled to interrogate.

As with all good playwrights, Peta's text does a lot of work for us: her language captures her characters, their universe, their dilemmas and informs the context. When the creative team broached the show's design, it felt important to create an environment that allowed for these frictions to be in constant, uninhibited play: a space that offers clues but which we as audience members would have to complete in our imaginations.

It may have been difficult to create the piece without Peta's long-standing experiences as an outreach worker and her complex understanding of this world. She would be the first to downplay it and would certainly never claim that her knowledge approximates those who live it every day. Her respect and appreciation of her characters' strength, humour and vitality give *Ugly Mugs* a great authenticity. But it's her simple desire for people to understand what goes on that gives it so much integrity.

Malthouse Theatre commissioned Peta to write this play shortly after our first meeting. Once we'd seen a draft I spoke to my colleague Lee Lewis at Griffin Theatre Company, who said, 'Well, if our companies can't program this sort of work, who can?' We are lucky that our companies have the freedom to be responsive enough to take on curly, public subjects that need to be aired. Lucky also that we have the amazing medium of theatre to help us imagine what we may never experience, to be entertained while being provoked, and all in the company of great performers and writers.

Marion Potts

Peta Brady
Playwright, Performer

Peta Brady has performed in various television, film and theatre projects over the past twenty years. Her television credits include: *The Slap*, *Beaconsfield*, *Librarians*, *Rush*, *City Homocide*, *Kath & Kim*, *Neighbours* and *R.A.N. (Remote Area Nurse)*. Her favourite film project was *Mullet* by David Caesar. Theatre highlights include: for La Mama: *Save For Crying*, for which she was nominated for a 2011 Green Room Award for Best Actress in Independent Theatre; for Melbourne Workers Theatre: *The Call*; for HotHouse Theatre / Malthouse Theatre: *Love*, for which she received a 2005 Green Room Award (Gerda Nicolson Award for an Emerging Actor). Peta wrote and performed in *Strands* (nominated for the 2011 Green Room Award for Best Ensemble in Independent Theatre and was awarded the 2011 R E ROSS Trust Development Award) and *Status Update* (nominated for the 2010 Green Room Award for Best Female Actor and Best New Writing in Independent Theatre).

Marion Potts
Director

Marion Potts is Malthouse Theatre's Artistic Director. For Malthouse Theatre Marion has directed: *The Dragon, Hate, Wild Surmise, Blood Wedding, Meow Meow's Little Match Girl* and its return season at the Southbank Centre in London, *'Tis Pity She's a Whore, Sappho... in 9 fragments*; for Bell Shakespeare: *Venus & Adonis, King Lear, The Taming of the Shrew, Hamlet, Othello*; for Sydney Theatre Company: *The Wonderful World of Dissocia, Playgrounds, Volpone, Don Juan, Life After George, Cyrano de Bergerac, The Crucible, Navigating, Del Del, Closer, The Herbal Bed, What is the Matter With Mary Jane?, Pygmalion, Where Are We Now?, The Café Latte Kid, The Blessing, Two Weeks With The Queen*; for Melbourne Theatre Company: *Grace*; for State Theatre Company of South Australia: *Equus, The Torrents, Gary's House, A Number, The Goat, or Who Is Sylvia?*; for Queensland Theatre Company: *Constance Drinkwater and the Final Days of Somerset*. Marion has worked with many of the country's finest theatre companies and was most recently Bell Shakespeare's Associate Artistic Director, creating its development arm Mind's Eye. Marion was Resident Director for Sydney Theatre Company from 1995-1999. She curated the 2003 National Playwrights Conference, was a chairperson of World Interplay and a member of the Theatre Board of the Australia Council. Marion received the Helpmann Award for Best Direction of a Play (*The Goat, or Who Is Sylvia?*) in 2006.

Michael Hankin
Designer

Michael Hankin's credits for Griffin Theatre Company include: *Rust and Bone* and *The Ugly One*. Other recent theatre work includes: *Angels In America* for Belvoir, which was nominated for Best Stage Design at the 2013 Sydney Theatre Awards and the Australian Production Design Guild Awards; *247 Days* for Chunky Move / Malthouse Theatre which is touring the Netherlands in 2014; and *Dirty Rotten Scoundrels* for Theatre Royal. He designed the set and costumes for *The Dark Room*, which was nominated for Best Stage Design at the 2011 Sydney Theatre Awards, and *Fool For Love* for Belvoir; *Lord of the*

Flies for Malthouse Theatre and *Truckstop* for Q Theatre / Seymour Centre, which won Best Independent Stage Design at the 2012 Sydney Theatre Awards. For Sydney Chamber Opera: Michael has designed *The Lighthouse*, *In the Penal Colony* and *Through the Gates*; and he has assistant-designed productions for Opera Australia, The English National Opera, Sydney Theatre Company, Belvoir St Theatre, Malthouse Theatre, and The Gordon Frost Organisation. Michael's other theatre designs include: *The Boat People* for The Hayloft Project; *Songs For the Fallen* for Brisbane Festival / the Seymour Centre / Old Fitzroy Theatre; *Judith* for Pavilion Theatre; *Suddenly Last Summer* and *Women of Troy* for Cell Block Theatre, and the creative development of *King Lear* for Bell Shakespeare. In film, Michael was both Costume and Production Designer on *Reason to Smile* as well as Berlin's Crystal Bear Award winning short films, *Julian* and *The Amber Amulet*.

Lucy Birkinshaw
Lighting Designer

Lucy Birkinshaw graduated from WAAPA (Advanced Diploma of Lighting Design for Production and Performance) and Curtin University (Bachelor of Arts, Fine Arts) and is a co-founder of the Filament Design Group. Lucy's design work spans theatre, music theatre, concert lighting, opera, dance, film and television. Lucy's designs include: for Malthouse Theatre: *Opera XS*, *Happiness*, *Africa*; for Magnormos: *Flowerchildren*, *The Hatpin*, *Sondheim Triptych*, *A Jerry Herman Triptych*, *[Title of Show]*, *Life's a Circus*; for The Hayloft Project: *The Seizure*, *Delectable Shelter*, *Spring Awakening*; for Perth International Arts Festival: *Beck's Music Box 2009–2011*; for Perth Theatre Company: *The Pride*, *Taking Liberty*, *Matchmaker*, *Baby Boomer Blues*, *Dealer's Choice*; for Black Swan Theatre Company: *The Messiah*, *Woyzeck*, *Falling Petals*. Lucy is the resident lighting designer for Magnormos, an independent producer of musical theatre in Melbourne.

Darrin Verhagen
Sound Design

Darrin Verhagen has recently been composing and sound designing for various Daniel Schlusser productions: for Melbourne Festival: *M+M*; for Melbourne Theatre Company: *Menagerie*; for Malthouse Theatre: *The Histrionic*; for Bell Shakespeare / Chamber Made Opera: *Ophelia Doesn't Live Here Anymore*. Previous theatre credits include: for Malthouse Theatre: *Porn.Cake, Sappho... in 9 fragments, Kitten, Not Like Beckett*; for Melbourne Theatre Company: *Grace, Godzone, Madagascar, The Birthday Party*. Recent film soundtracks have included: *The Last Time I Saw Richard* by Nicholas Verso and *The Templer Journey*. His installations this year were *On View* for Sue Healey at Manly Art Gallery, *Audiokinetic Jukebox* for National Gallery of Victoria and *Music of the Spheres* for White Night. Darrin is a Senior Lecturer in sound and multisensory experience at the Audiokinetic Experiments (AkE) Lab, RMIT.

Margaret Harvey
Assistant Director

Margaret Harvey has had a prolific career as an actor working for companies such as Malthouse Theatre, Melbourne Theatre Company, Sydney Theatre Company, Belvoir, Queensland Theatre Company, Black Swan Theatre Company and Deckchair Theatre. More recently she made her film directing debut on *The Hunter*, a short film selected at last year's Melbourne International Film Festival which went on to play at Brisbane International Film Festival, Adelaide Film Festival, Flickerfest and imagineNATIVE Film Festival in Toronto. She has written, directed and produced four documentaries for NITV. In 2012 through Multicultural Arts Victoria she co-produced and facilitated the making of *Ubuzima Bushasha (new life)* which screened at ACMI. Margaret has worked on numerous music clips including Blue King Brown's 'Women's Revolution'. For theatre she recently directed: for Wominjeka Festival: *HUNTED*; for Ilbijerri Theatre: *Tiddalik* and *Body Armour*, which toured nationally. In 2008 she was awarded a fellowship from the Australia Council for the Arts in which she began to explore a process for telling and creating Torres Strait Island stories for the stage. She is now undertaking a PhD through Monash University and she continues to collaborate with her brother John Harvey, through Brown Cab Productions.

Isabella Kerdijk
Stage Manager

Isabella Kerdijk's credits for Griffin Theatre Company include: *And No More Shall We Part*, *This Year's Ashes*. Other theatre credits include: for Opera Australia on Sydney Harbour: *Carmen* (Production Coordinator); for Circus Oz: *Cranked Up* (Assistant Stage Manager); for Ensemble Theatre: *Rainman*, *The Ruby Sunrise* (Assistant Stage Manager); for Belvoir: *Stories I Want to Tell You in Person*, *20 Questions*, *Thyestes* (European tour). For First Stage Productions: *Woman*; for Legs on the Wall: *Bubble* (Assistant Stage Manager); for NIDA Open Program: *A Midsummer Night's Dream*. Other credits include: *The Mousetrap Australia / NZ tour*; for The Garden of Unearthly Delights: *Spiegeltent* (Venue Manager); Sydney Festival; Woodford Folk Festival; Production Manager for Puppetry of the Penis and Stage Manager for *Empire* for Spiegelworld. Isabella trained at NIDA.

Harry Borland
Performer

Harry Borland made his first public appearance in the theatrical event *Death by Chocolate* for WhoDunnit Events / 2007 Melbourne Fringe Festival, which won that year's Best Special Event Award. In 2009 Harry played the titular role in the short film *My Girlfriend Jim* as well as appearing in *At the Formal*. Other short film credits include: *Spit*, *Junior* and *Poppy Projectionist*. Harry's first lead role in a feature film was *The Playbook* which was chosen to open the LDS Film Festival in Salt Lake City, Utah. Most recently he appeared in *The Turning* based on Tim Winton's short stories, and the short film *Emo: The Musical* which premiered at the Berlin Film Festival. *Ugly Mugs* is Harry's stage debut.

Steve Le Marquand
Performer

Steve Le Marquand's credits for Griffin Theatre Company include: *Songket* and *The Return*. His other theatre credits include: for Belvoir / Melbourne Theatre Company / Queensland Theatre Company: *Summer Of The Seventeenth Doll*; for Belvoir: *Death Of A Salesman*, *Paul*, *The Spook*, *Buried Child*, *Waiting For Godot*; for Sydney Theatre Company as part of the Actors' Company: *War Of The Roses*, *Gallipoli*, *Holy Day*, *The Serpent's Teeth*, *Tales from the Vienna Woods*; for Melbourne Theatre Company / Sydney Theatre Company: *Don's Party*. He co-wrote, produced, directed and starred in the hugely successful theatre production *He Died with a Felafel in His Hand*. For film, Steve has been seen in *A Few Best Men*, *Beneath Hill 60*, *Last Train to Freo*, *Razzle Dazzle: A Journey into Dance*, *Men's Group*, *Kokoda*, *Lost Things*, *Mullet*, *South Pacific*, *Two Hands* and *Vertical Limit*. Steve has also appeared in various award-winning short films including *Cliché*, *Bomb* and *Franswa Sharl*. Television credits include *Wentworth*, *Old School*, *Rake*, *The Moodys*, *Small Time Gangster*, *Underbelly: Razor*, *Sea Patrol*, *Laid*, *All Saints*, *Farscape*, *Young Lions*, *A Difficult Woman*, *Backberner*, *Blue Heelers*, *Wildside*, *G.P.*, *Murder Call*, *Big Sky*, *Water Rats*, *Soldier Soldier*, *Home and Away* and *Police Rescue*.

Sara West
Performer

Sara West's credits for Griffin Theatre Company include: *Dreams in White* and *Heartbreak Hotel*. Her other theatre credits include: for Sydney Theatre Company: *Travelling North*; for Belvoir: *Babyteeth*. Film credits include: *Dirt Girls*, which she also wrote and directed, *One Eyed Girl* and *The Turned*. Short films include *Collision*, *Touch*, *Spine* and *Hey Joe*. Television credits include *ANZAC Girls*. Short film directing credits include *River Water*. Sara graduated from the Flinders Drama Centre in 2010.

ABOUT GRIFFIN THEATRE COMPANY

Griffin Theatre Company is Australia's new writing theatre. We develop and stage the best Australian stories, for the widest possible audience.

For more than 30 years, the Griffin mission has been to bring our audiences the highest standards of theatrical craft. We also have a passion for developing Australian talent, with many of our nation's most celebrated artists starting their professional careers with us.

Griffin produces an annual subscription season of four to five Main Season shows by Australian playwrights, and co-presents a season of new work with leading independent artists. We also support artists through professional development opportunities, including artist residencies and masterclasses.

Our home is the historic SBW Stables Theatre, a thriving cultural hub and Sydney's most intimate and persuasive space for actors and audiences to meet. We hope to see you here soon.

GRIFFIN THEATRE COMPANY
13 CRAIGEND ST
KINGS CROSS NSW 2011

PHONE 02 9332 1052
FAX 02 9331 1524

INFO@GRIFFINTHEATRE.COM.AU
WWW.GRIFFINTHEATRE.COM.AU

SBW STABLES THEATRE
10 NIMROD ST
KINGS CROSS NSW 2011

BOOKINGS
GRIFFINTHEATRE.COM.AU
02 9361 3817

113 Sturt Street, Southbank
Victoria 3006, Australia
BOX OFFICE +61 3 9685 5111

ABOUT MALTHOUSE THEATRE

Innovative and internationally recognised, Malthouse Theatre is Melbourne's home of contemporary theatre. Using high-octane performance as its currency, Malthouse Theatre presents an adventurous annual program of works as provocative as they are fun, as visceral as they are affirming, and always a little irreverent.

BOARD OF DIRECTORS
Michele Levine (Chair), John Daley (Deputy Chair), Frankie Airey, Ian McRae, Sarah Morgan, Nick Schlieper, Thea Snow, Sigrid Thornton, Kerri Turner, Leonard Vary

Artistic Director
Marion Potts

Executive Producer
Sarah Neal

Associate Artist (Composition)
David Chisholm

Associate Artist (Writing)
Lally Katz

Associate Artist (Direction)
Matthew Lutton

Dramaturg
Mark Pritchard

Female Director in Residence
Clare Watson

Indigenous Engagement
Jason Tamiru

Associate Producer
Josh Wright

Administrator
Narda Shanley

Finance Manager
Mario Agostinoni

Finance Administrator
Liz White

Marketing & Communications Manager
Lisa Scicluna

Media Manager
Maria O'Dwyer

Digital Strategy & Marketing Coordinator
Alice Gage

Communications Coordinator
Emily Fiori

Graphic Designer
Jane Roberts

Company Manager
Alice Muhling

Development Manager
Rachel Petchesky

Development Coordinator
Kim Brockett

Building Manager
Peter Mandersloot

Ticketing Manager
Emma Quinn

Assistant Ticketing Manager
Lauren White

Executive Assistant
Nicole Benson

Production Manager
David Miller

Technical Manager
Baird McKenna

Operations Manager
Dexter Varley

Head of Lighting
Stephen Hawker

Head Mechanist
Andy Moore

Theatre Technician
Nathanael Bristow

Head of Wardrobe
Delia Spicer

Workshop Supervisor
David Craig

Steel Fabricator
Goffredo Mameli

Front of House Managers
Sean Ladhams, Anita Posterino

Bar Manager
Cherry Rivers

facebook.com/MalthouseTheatre
@MalthouseMelb
@MalthouseTheatre

malthousetheatre.com.au

ACTORS EQUITY TURNS 75

For the last 75 years Actors Equity has been the home of Australia's professional performers.

Equity has campaigned and lobbied for the kind of industry we want to be a part of - one that treats performers with respect and values local content; one in which culture thrives and art is celebrated for art's sake.

Griffin is proud to join Equity in celebrating 75 years of activism and achievement.

"HAPPY 75TH BIRTHDAY EQUITY. THANKS FOR LETTING ME BE A MEMBER FOR THE PAST 23 OF THOSE YEARS.

FOR ME, BEING A MEMBER OF EQUITY MEANS THERE'S SOMEONE TO CALL WHEN THINGS DON'T SEEM RIGHT WITH THE JOB. THAT SOMEONE ON THE END OF THE LINE WILL BE ABLE TO ANSWER MY QUESTIONS OR LOOK INTO THE FAIRNESS OF A SITUATION AND ADVISE ME. IT MEANS I RECEIVE RESIDUALS AND THAT THERE IS A STANDARD RATE AT WHICH I SHOULDN'T BE PAID BELOW.

I BASICALLY FEEL LIKE I'VE GOT MY BACK COVERED WITH MY EQUITY CARD."

Peta Brady Writer and cast member of Ugly Mugs & proud Equity member since 1991

GTC
RHO
IEM
FAP
FTA
IRN
NEY

GRIFFIN STAFF

Patron
Seaborn, Broughton and Walford Foundation

Griffin acknowledges the generosity of the Seaborn, Broughton and Walford Foundation in allowing it the use of the SBW Stables Theatre rent free, less outgoings, since 1986.

Artistic Director
Lee Lewis

Associate Artist
Ben Winspear

Administration & Program Coordinator
Melanie Carolan

Development Manager
Will Harvey

General Manager
Simon Wellington

Deputy General Manager
Viv Rosman

Board
Bruce Meagher (Chair)
Sophie McCarthy (Deputy Chair)
Lee Lewis
Kate Mulvany
Nikki Barrett
Tim Duggan
Patrick Guerrera
Simone Whetton

Production Manager
Glenn Dulihanty

Production Coordinator
Ulli Briese

Financial Consultant
Tracey Whitby

Marketing Manager
Kristy Mayhew

Digital & Social Media Manager
Stephanie Hui

Publicist
Emma Collison

Studio Artists
Mary Rachel Brown
Jennifer Medway
Lachlan Philpott
Luke Rogers

Affiliate Directors
Constantine Costi
Elsie Edgerton-Till

Bookkeeper
Kylie Richards

Box Office Manager
Elliott Wilshier

Bar Manager
Damien Storer

Resident Artist
Sopa Enari

Writers Under Commission
Kit Brookman (A Rabbit for Kim Jong-Il)
Declan Greene
Maxine Mellor (The Silver Alps)
Michele Lee (Moths)

Front of House & Bar Supervisors
Julian Larnach
Luke Rogers
Liv Satchell

Web Developer
Holly

Brand and Graphic Design
RE:

Cover Photography
Brett Boardman

GRIFFIN DONORS

Income from Griffin activities covers less than 40% of our operating costs – leaving an ever increasing gap for us to fill through government funding, sponsorship and the generosity of our individual supporters. Your support helps us bridge the gap, keep ticket prices affordable and our work at its best. To make a donation and a difference, contact Griffin on 9332 1052 or donate online at griffintheatre.com.au

Commission $12,500+
Darin Cooper Family
Anthony & Suzanne Maple-Brown

Production $10,000+
Anonymous (1)
Sophie McCarthy & Antony Green

Studio $5,000
James Emmett & Peter Wilson
Gil Appleton
The Goodness Foundation
Limb Family Foundation
The Sky Foundation
Rhonda McIver
Geoff & Wendy Simpson
Danielle Smith

Workshop $1,000-$4,999
Anonymous (5)
Alex Byrne & Sue Hearn
Richard & Elizabeth Longes
Dr Gae M Anderson
Bernard Coles
Richard Cottrell
Ros & Paul Espie
Peter Graves
Larry & Tina Grumley
Margaret Johnston
Stephen Manning
Dr Stephen McNamara
Ian Neuss & Penny Young
Dr David Nguyen
Anthony Paull
Chris & Fran Roberts
Jane Thorn
Paul & Jennifer Winch
Russ & Rae Cottle
Sian Jenkins
Christopher Tooher
Merilyn Sleigh & Raoul de Ferranti

Reading $500-$999
Anonymous (4)
Wendy Ashton
Jan Barham
Andrew Bovell
Alex Bowen & Catherine Sullivan
Angela Bowne
David Caulfield
Michael & Colleen Chesterman
Peter Demou
Elizabeth Evatt
Jono Gavin
Susan Hyde
Henry Johnston
Bill & Elaine McLaughlin
Natalie Pelham
Diana Simmonds
Isla Tooth
Louise Walsh & Dave Jordan
Wendy Elder
Katharine Brisbane
G James Hartwright
Libby Higgin
Abraham Hammoud
Deena Shiff & Jim Gillespie
Maggies Thai
Simone & Anna Whetton
Rose Hiscock
Michele Lee
Judy & Sam Weiss
Michael Hobbs
Jennifer Ledgar & Bob Lim

First Draft $200-$499
Anonymous (5)
Jes Andersen
Corinne & Bryan Everts
Jan Chapman
Max Dingle
Eric Dole
Stephen Farr
Gadens Lawyers
Janet Heffernan
Danielle Hoareau
Alexandra Joel & Philip Mason
Beverley Johnson
Maria & Ross Kelly
Dr Daniel Levin
Ian & Elizabeth MacDonald
Duncan McKay
Sarah Miller
Neville Mitchell
Liz Nield
Gerard Neiditsche & Marcus Da Silva
Sally Patten
William Penhale
Lachlan Philpott
Pip Rath
Alex O Redmond
Barbara Richardson
Catherine Rothery
Dianne & David Russell
Yvonne Sebesfi
Michelle Shek
Jann Skinner
Ross Steele
Ros Tarsziss
Robyn Ayres
Vodafone Foundation
Pamela Bennett
Cyril J Keightley
Ross Kelly
Annie Page
Ann Robinson
Robyn Tantau
Frank Messina
Gemma Rygate
Prof Peter Shergold
Neil Thompson
Simon Chan – Art Atrium
Dr Caroline Hong
Vera Hong
Wendy Buswell
Linda Newton
Jo Grisard
Irena Nebenzahl
Janet Grant
Priscilla Adey

We would also like to thank Peter O'Connell for his expertise, guidance and time.

Current as of 20/06/2014

GRIFFIN FUND

The Griffin Fund is a new initiative focusing on education programs, leadership pathways for artists, touring Griffin productions and international exchange opportunities. Donations to the Fund are pledged for a three-year period. It is an investment in the future prospects of the company and the artists we work with. For more information please visit griffintheatre.com.au/support-us or contact the Development Manager on 9332 1052.

Founding Donors
Anonymous (1)
Baly Douglas Foundation
John Bell & Anna Volska
Michael & Charmaine Bradley
Nathan Bennet & Yael Perry
Ange Cecco & Melanie Bienemann
Alison Deans & Kevin Powell
Catherine Dovey and Kim Williams
Lilian & Ken Horler
Lee Lewis & Brett Boardman
Ross Lewin
Bruce Meagher & Greg Waters
Sophie McCarthy & Antony Green
Pip Rath & Wayne Lonergran
Peter & Dianne O'Connell
Ian Phipps
Ian Robertson
Will Sheehan
Stuart Thomas
Simon Wellington & Sanjeev Kumar
Annabel Ritchie
Louise Walsh & Dave Jordan
Peter Ingle
Mary Holt

GRIFFIN SPONSORS

Griffin would like to thank the following:

Government Supporters

Patron

2014 Season Sponsor

Production Sponsors

Associate Sponsors

Foundations and Trusts

Company Sponsors

Griffin Theatre Company is assisted by the Australian Government through the Australia Council, its arts funding and advisory body; and the NSW Government through Arts NSW.

www.currency.com.au

Visit Currency Press' website now to:

- Buy your books online
- Browse through our full list of titles, from plays to screenplays, books on theatre, film and music, and more
- Choose a play for your school or amateur performance group by cast size and gender
- Obtain information about performance rights
- Find out about theatre productions and other performing arts news across Australia
- For students, read our study guides
- For teachers, access syllabus and other relevant information
- Sign up for our email newsletter

The performing arts publisher

www.ingramcontent.com/pod-product-compliance
Lightning Source LLC
Chambersburg PA
CBHW050021090426
42734CB00021B/3369